What Do Christians Believe?

What are the key doctrines of the Christian faith? The core teachings of the Bible have defined Christianity for 2,000 years. Virtually all Christians who seek to have a faith that is biblical hold to some form of these basic doctrines. Christians may not always agree on how they work out the details of their faith, but they should agree on the essential doctrines, these core truths.

In essentials, unity; in non-essentials, liberty, and in all things, charity.[1]

We can identify the essential doctrines of the Christian faith by looking at the core truth of the Gospel, which is the salvation of humanity through the life, death, and resurrection of Jesus Christ. Salvation, as God has revealed to us through his Holy Scriptures, is defined as forgiveness of sins and everlasting life with God by confessing that "Jesus is Lord" and believing that God raised Jesus from the dead (Romans 10:9). By examining the Gospel message, we can identify 14 doctrines that are necessary for salvation to be possible.

What Are the Essential Doctrines?

The essential doctrines of Christianity have to do with
- who God is,
- who Jesus Christ is,
- God's love for people, and his desire to save them.

Below are the 14 essential salvation doctrines that have to be true in order for anyone to know God and be saved:

1) God's Unity
2) God's Tri-unity
3) Human Depravity
4) Christ's Virgin Birth
5) Christ's Sinlessness
6) Christ's Deity
7) Christ's Humanity
8) The Necessity of God's Grace
9) The Necessity of Faith
10) Christ's Atoning Death
11) Christ's Bodily Resurrection
12) Christ's Bodily Ascension
13) Christ's Intercession
14) Christ's Second Coming

In addition, two more essentials define how we know about salvation:

15) Inspiration of Scripture
16) Method of Interpretation

[1] Rupertus Meldenius (AD 1627)

Key Christian Beliefs

Essential Doctrine
Made Easy

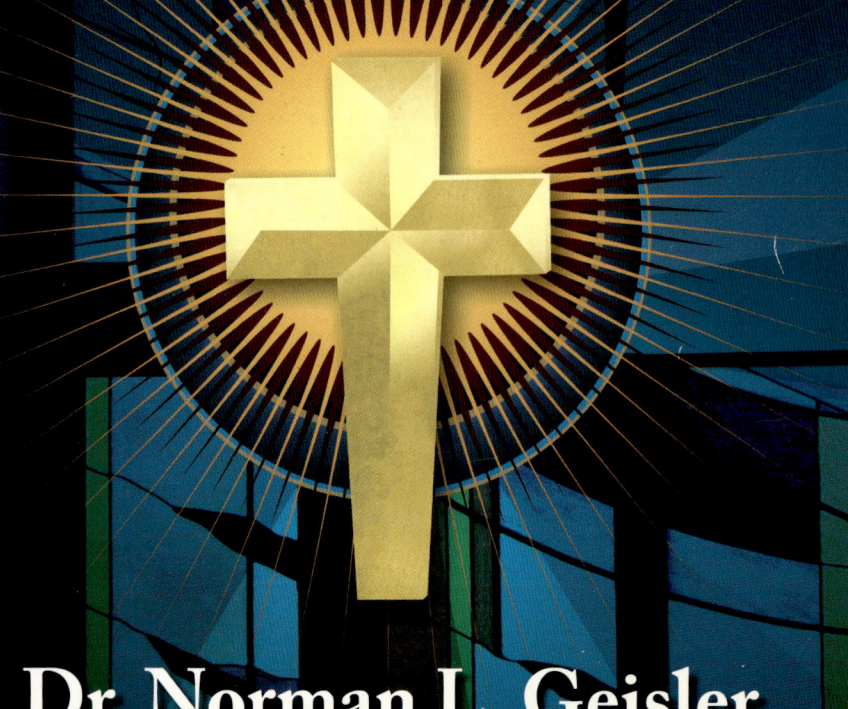

Dr. Norman L. Geisler

ROSE PUBLISHING

What Do I Actually Need to Believe?
We are sinful and cannot please God by our own good works alone. We can never be "good enough."

What's at Stake Here?
When we try to deal with the problem of separation and death on our own terms, we will fail, resulting in eternal separation from God.

As it is written: "There is no one righteous, not even one; there is no one who understands, no one who seeks God. All have turned away, they have together become worthless; there is no one who does good, not even one." —Romans 3:10, 11

4 CHRIST'S VIRGIN BIRTH

Jesus was born as a result of a miracle: Mary, Jesus' mother, became pregnant without ever having sexual relations. The doctrine of Jesus' Virgin Birth is not primarily about Mary's virginity and miraculous conception. Though this miracle fulfilled a preordained prophecy (Isaiah 7:14), the reason it is essential has to do with God's supernatural intervention. Our sin is not merely something we do—it is who we are. It is inborn. Our depravity is transmitted to us from our parents (Psalm 51:5; 1 Corinthians. 15:22; Romans 5:12-15). Because God interrupted the natural birth process in the case of Jesus, Jesus did not inherit a sin nature. In other words, Jesus not only did not sin, he had no inclination to sin even when tempted. He was perfect.

What Do I Actually Need to Believe?
Jesus became a human being through a supernatural conception in Mary's womb.

What's at Stake Here?
God's supernatural intervention in order to break the chain of sin.

This is how the birth of Jesus Christ came about: His mother Mary was pledged to be married to Joseph, but before they came together, she was found to be with child through the Holy Spirit…. [An angel said]: "Joseph son of David, do not be afraid to take Mary home as your wife, because what is conceived in her is from the Holy Spirit. She will give birth to a son, and you are to give him the name Jesus, because he will save his people from their sins." All this took place to fulfill what the Lord had said through the prophet: "The virgin will be with child and will give birth to a son, and they will call him Immanuel"—which means, "God with us." —Matthew 1:18-23

5 CHRIST'S SINLESSNESS

Christ was born of a virgin, and he did not suffer the effects of a sin nature.
Throughout his life Jesus remained sinless. Because of our sin, we could not have a relationship with God; but because Jesus did not sin he was perfectly able to represent us (stand in our place) before God.

What Do I Actually Need to Believe?
Jesus was perfect.

How Do We Know About Essential Doctrines?

We know about the essential doctrines through the Bible; however, the inspiration of Scripture as a doctrine is not necessary for salvation to be possible. People were saved before there was a Bible, and some people are saved without ever reading the Bible. The Bible is, however, the only divinely authoritative foundation that makes the plan of salvation *knowable*.

15 INSPIRATION OF SCRIPTURE

In order for us to have a sure foundation for what we believe, God revealed his Word (the Bible) as the basis of our beliefs. As Thomas Aquinas put it, "in order that salvation might the easier be brought to man and be more certain, it was necessary that men be instructed concerning divine matters through divine revelation," which is the Bible (Summa Theologica 1.1.1). God cannot err (Hebrews 6:18) and neither can his Word (John 17:17). Without a divinely authoritative revelation from God, such as we have in the Scriptures, we could never be sure of the doctrines that are necessary for salvation.

16 METHOD OF INTERPRETATION

In addition, all the salvation doctrines are derived from the Bible by the literal method of interpretation—that is, Scripture is true, just as the author meant it. By applying the historical-grammatical method of interpretation to Scripture one can know *which* truths are essential for salvation.

To Believe or Not to Believe?

Not all doctrines necessary for salvation are necessary for a person to believe in order to be saved. There is a distinct difference between what must be *true* in order for us to be saved and what must be *believed* in order for us to be saved. For instance, nowhere does the Bible say it is necessary to believe in the Virgin Birth in order to get into heaven; nonetheless, the Virgin Birth assures us that God took an active role in breaking the bonds of sin through his Son, Jesus.

There are certain essential doctrines that one may not believe and still be saved (for example, the Virgin Birth, Ascension of Christ, the Second Coming), and there are certain things one *must* believe in order to be saved. A person must believe that Christ died for sins and rose again (Romans 10:9; 1 Corinthians 15:1-6). One must "believe in the Lord Jesus Christ" (Acts 16:31). Since the word "Lord" (*kurios*) when it refers to Christ in the New Testament means "deity," one cannot deny the deity of Christ and be saved (Acts 2:21, 36; 3:14-16; 5:30-35; 10:39; 1 Corinthians 12:3).

...If you confess with your mouth, "Jesus is Lord," and believe in your heart that God raised him from the dead, you will be saved. For it is with your heart that you believe and are justified, and it is with your mouth that you confess and are saved. As the Scripture says, "Anyone who trusts in him will never be put to shame." —Romans 10: 9-11

What Do I Actually Need to Believe?
Jesus is coming again soon, and we should be ready.

What's at Stake Here?
Our hope of being together with Christ.

At that time the sign of the Son of Man will appear in the sky, and all the nations of the earth will mourn. They will see the Son of Man coming on the clouds of the sky, with power and great glory. —Matthew 24:30

Behold, I am coming soon! My reward is with me, and I will give to everyone according to what he has done. —Revelation 22:12

For you died, and your life is now hidden with Christ in God. When Christ, who is your life, appears, then you also will appear with him in glory. —Colossians 3:3, 4

You also must be ready, because the Son of Man will come at an hour when you do not expect him. —Luke 12:40

After Jesus returns, believers will enter conscious eternal blessing and unbelievers will go into conscious eternal punishment.

Eternal Life

Do not let your hearts be troubled. Trust in God; trust also in me. In my Father's house are many rooms; if it were not so, I would have told you. I am going there to prepare a place for you. And if I go and prepare a place for you I will come back and take you to be with me that you also may be where I am. —John 14:1-3

Now we see but a poor reflection as in a mirror; then we shall see face to face. Now I know in part; then I shall know fully, even as I am fully known. —1 Corinthians 13:12

He will wipe every tear from their eyes. There will be no more death or mourning or crying or pain, for the old order of things has passed away. —Revelation 21:4

Eternal Separation

This will happen when the Lord Jesus is revealed from heaven in blazing fire with his powerful angels. He will punish those who do not know God and do not obey the gospel of our Lord Jesus. They will be punished with everlasting destruction and shut out from the presence of the Lord and from the majesty of his power. —2 Thessalonians 1:7-9

Then I saw a great white throne and him who was seated on it. Earth and sky fled from his presence, and there was no place for them. And I saw the dead, great and small, standing before the throne.... The dead were judged according to what they had done.... Then death and Hades were thrown into the lake of fire. If anyone's name was not found written in the book of life, he was thrown into the lake of fire. —Revelation 20:11-15

What's at Stake Here?
The ability of Christ to represent us before God and thus provide salvation for us.

God made him who had no sin to be sin for us.... —2 Corinthians 5:21

For we ... have one who has been tempted in every way, just as we are—yet was without sin. —Hebrews 4:15

He committed no sin, and no deceit was found in his mouth. —1 Peter 2:22

6 CHRIST'S DEITY
The only way for humans to be restored spiritually to God was for God to build a bridge across the gap of separation. So God, while retaining his full God nature, became a perfect man in Christ in order to bridge the chasm. If he is not both God and Man he cannot mediate between God and man (1 Timothy 2:5). Jesus Christ is the second Person in the Trinity.

What Do I Actually Need to Believe?
Jesus Christ is, in essence, God. He is divine, not just a good teacher or a righteous man.

What's at Stake Here?
Jesus' ability to save us.

In the beginning was the Word, and the Word was with God, and the Word was God. —John 1:1

For in Christ all the fullness of the deity lives in bodily form. —Colossians 2:9

But about the Son he says, "Your throne, O God, will last for ever and ever." —Hebrews 1:8

7 CHRIST'S HUMANITY
Jesus was also fully human. Jesus got tired; he slept; he sweated; he got hungry and thirsty. Without being fully human, Jesus could not pay the price for human sin. He needed to be divine to have the power to *save* us, and he needed to be human in order to adequately *represent* us. Christ had to be both divine and human.

What Do I Actually Need to Believe?
Jesus Christ was fully human, as well as fully divine.

What's at Stake Here?
Confidence in Jesus' ability to fully represent humankind in atonement.

The Word became flesh and made his dwelling among us. —John 1:14

The Essential Doctrines in the Creeds

The essential doctrines are reflected in the Church's ancient statements of faith called "creeds." Creeds are short summaries of what the Bible teaches.

The Apostles' Creed
The Apostles' Creed was one of the earliest statements of faith crafted by Christian leaders to clarify basic beliefs. All 14 essential salvation doctrines are contained in it. Each doctrine is indicated by bracketed numbers: [9] = Essential Doctrine #9.

I believe [9] in God [1], the Father Almighty, the Creator of heaven and earth, and in Jesus Christ, his only Son, our Lord [6]: Who was conceived of the Holy Spirit [2], born of the Virgin Mary [4, 5], suffered [10] under Pontius Pilate, was crucified, died [7], and was buried. (He descended into hell.) The third day he arose again from the dead [11]. He ascended into heaven [12] and sits at the right hand of God the Father [13] Almighty, from whence he shall come to judge the living and the dead [14]. I believe in the Holy Spirit, the holy catholic [universal] church, the communion of saints, the forgiveness [8] of sins [3], the resurrection of the flesh, and life everlasting [14]. Amen.

—The Apostles Creed

The Nicene Creed
In addition to the 14 essential salvation doctrines, the Nicene Creed makes reference to Scripture as the basis for the Creeds. Scripture is the method through which essential doctrines are revealed.

Athanasian Creed
The Athanasian Creed emphasizes the deity of Christ and the Trinity. In addition, the Athanasian Creed was directed against many heresies such as Tritheism (belief in three Gods), Monophysitism (belief in the "confusion" or co-mingling of the two natures), Nestorianism (belief that the two natures are independent or loosely united), Arianism (belief that Jesus is created and not divine), Adoptionism (belief that Jesus was merely a man who was adopted into the Godhead as Son), Apollinarianism (belief that Jesus is partially human), Annihilationism (belief that some souls are destroyed), and Universalism (belief that everyone will be saved).

The Creed of Chalcedon
In addition to the other essentials, the Chalcedonian Creed stresses the Triune Godhead, the Virgin Birth of Christ, Jesus' humanity and deity, as well as the eternity of the Son before all time.

1 GOD'S UNITY

There is only one God. He has always existed and will always exist. There is one—and only one—God, Creator of the universe.

What Do I Actually Need to Believe?
There is only one God.

What's at Stake Here?
Knowing the only true God (John 17:3).

Glossary

Ascension—Being taken up; Christ was taken up by God into heaven after the Resurrection.
Atonement—To cover, cancel, or forgive sins.
Creed—Summary of beliefs or faith statements held in common by a group.
Deity—Godhood; having the nature of God.
Depravity—Humans' natural bent toward sin (see Genesis 3; 1 Corinthians 15:22; Romans 5:12-15).
Doctrine—Formal teaching.
Eternal—Forever; outside of time and space.
Grace—Undeserved favor; God's mercy.
High Priest—One who represents the people of God to God. In ancient Israel, there was only one high priest chosen to represent the entire nation before God in worship. (See *Mediator*.)
Historical-grammatical method—Method of interpreting Scripture which centers on the historical context and the grammatical interpretation of a text.
Incarnation—Jesus' assumption of human nature; His becoming a human being in a specific time and place.
Inspiration (of Scripture)—Supernatural influence that gives God's authority to a human writing.
Intercession—Prayer or intervention on behalf of another.
Mediator—Go-between; one who intervenes between two parties to bring reconciliation.
Orthodoxy—"Right belief" as opposed to "heresy" (wrong belief).
Prophecy—To accurately predict an event or situation.
Redemption—To buy back or redeem.
Resurrection—God's action in bringing a dead body back to life.
Righteousness—Being in right relationship with God and man.
Salvation—God's work that delivers us from the consequences of our sin.
Sin—To "miss the mark"; failing. A deviation or transgression of God's will.
Rebellion—the condition of fallen man (depravity); a willful transgression of a known law of God. It is what separates mankind from God and reaps the result of guilt and eternal condemnation. "The wages of sin is death..."(Romans 6:23).
Soteriology—Branch of theology dealing with the doctrine of salvation.
Trinity or Tri-unity—Tri = three; unity = one. Describes the nature of the one God who is also three Persons.

Resources

Bettenson, Henry and Chris Maunder, eds. *Documents of the Christian Church*. 3rd Edition. New York: Oxford University Press, 1999.

Enns, Paul. *Moody Handbook of Theology*. Chicago: Moody, 1989.

Geisler, Norman L. *Systematic Theology*, Vol. 1. *Prolegomena and Bibliology*. Minneapolis: Bethany House Pub., 2002.

_____. *Systematic Theology*, Vol. 2. *God and Creation*. Minneapolis: Bethany House Pub., 2003.

_____. *Systematic Theology*, Vol. 3. *Sin and Salvation*. Minneapolis: Bethany House Pub., 2004.

_____. *Systematic Theology*, Vol. 4. *Church and Last Things*. Minneapolis: Bethany House Pub., 2005.

House, H. Wayne. *Charts of Christian Theology & Doctrine*. Grand Rapids: Zondervan, 1992.

Ryrie, Charles. *Survey of Bible Doctrine*. Chicago: Moody, 1989.

Schaff, Philip. *Creeds of Christendom*. Vol. 2. *Greek and Latin Creeds*. New York: Harper & Brothers, 1931.

What's at Stake Here?
The Holy Spirit's work in the life of the believer.

But I tell you the truth: It is for your good that I am going away. Unless I go away, the Counselor [Holy Spirit] will not come to you; but if I go, I will send him to you. —John 16:7

When he had led them out to the vicinity of Bethany, he lifted up his hands and blessed them. While he was blessing them, he left them and was taken up into heaven. —Luke 24:50, 51

After he said this, he was taken up before their very eyes, and a cloud hid him from their sight. They were looking intently up into the sky as he was going. —Acts 1:9-10

13 Christ's Intercession

Christ's bodily ascension allowed him to serve as our mediator (or high priest) before God. In God's presence, Christ prays continually on our behalf. Like a lawyer defends someone before a judge, so Jesus defends us before the bar of God's law and against the accusations of Satan (Revelation 12:10).

What Do I Actually Need to Believe?
Christ represents our best interests before God.

What's at Stake Here?
Assurance that my prayers are heard by God.

After he had provided purification for sins, he sat down at the right hand of the Majesty in heaven. —Hebrews 1:3

For we do not have a high priest who is unable to sympathize with our weaknesses, but we have one who has been tempted in every way, just as we are—yet without sin. —Hebrews 4:15

Therefore he is able to save completely those who come to God through him, because he always lives to intercede for them. —Hebrews 7:25

But if anybody does sin, we have one who speaks to the Father in our defense—Jesus Christ, the Righteous One. —1 John 2:1

14 Christ's Second Coming

Just as Christ left the world physically, so he will return in the same manner. His second coming is the hope of the world. When he returns, dead believers will receive their resurrected bodies. Believers that are alive when he returns will not die, but will be transformed into immortal, physical bodies. Christ's bodily return to earth will be visible to all, and believers will rule with him in his kingdom and live with him forever. Those who do not believe will be separated from God's goodness forever.

Christ Jesus: . . . taking the very nature of a servant, being made in human likeness. . . . —Philippians 2:7, 8

Since the children have flesh and blood, he too shared in their humanity so that by his death he might destroy him who holds the power of death—that is, the devil. . . . —Hebrews 2:14

8 THE NECESSITY OF GOD'S GRACE

Because of human depravity, we cannot save ourselves. It is by God's grace alone that salvation is possible. God is right to call humankind to account for sin. However, by his grace, undeserving people will be united in fellowship with him and avoid judgment. Without God's grace, no one could come into relationship with God. Relationship with God is peace, joy, and eternal life itself (John 17:3).

What Do I Actually Need to Believe?
God—and God alone—is able to rescue us.

What's at Stake Here?
Our relationship to God, eternal life.

For it is by grace you have been saved, through faith—and this not from yourselves, it is the gift of God—not by works, so that no one can boast. —Ephesians 2:8, 9

If a man remains in me and I in him, he will bear much fruit; apart from me you can do nothing. —John 15:5

He saved us, not because of righteous things we had done, but because of his mercy. —Titus 3:5-7

It does not, therefore, depend on man's desire or effort, but on God's mercy. —Romans 9:16

9 THE NECESSITY OF FAITH

Faith is trusting that God can and will save us. No one can earn salvation. No amount of good works can ever repay the debt that is owed to God. However, by trusting in him and thankfully accepting his gift of salvation, we can be united with God. Faith is an act on our part, but it is not a work. Faith is trusting God to do what we could not do for ourselves (Ephesians 2:8, 9; Titus 3:5).

What Do I Actually Need to Believe?
That faith, not works, connects us to God.

What's at Stake Here?
Whether we want to be judged by what we deserve or with God's undeserved favor (grace).

And without faith it is impossible to please God, because anyone who comes to him must believe that he exists and that he rewards those who earnestly seek him. —Hebrews 11:6

However, to the man who does not work but trusts God who justifies the wicked, his faith is credited as righteousness. —Romans 4:5

How Other Religious Groups Treat these Essentials

	Latter Day Saints (Mormonism)	Jehovah's Witnesses (Watchtower)	Scientology	Christian Science
1) God's Unity	Deny	Accept	Deny	Deny
2) God's Tri-unity	Deny	Deny	Deny	Deny
3) Human Depravity	Redefine	Accept	Deny	Deny
4) Christ's Virgin Birth	Redefine	Accept	Deny	Deny
5) Christ's Sinlessness	Accept	Accept	Deny	Redefine
6) Christ's Deity	Deny	Deny	Deny	Deny
7) Christ's Humanity	Redefine	Accept	Redefine	Redefine
8) The Necessity of God's Grace	Redefine	Redefine	Deny	Deny
9) The Necessity of Faith	Redefine	Redefine	Deny	Deny
10) Christ's Atoning Death	Redefine	Redefine	Deny	Deny
11) Christ's Bodily Resurrection	Accept	Deny	Deny	Deny
12) Christ's Bodily Ascension	Accept	Deny	Deny	Deny
13) Christ's Intercession	Accept	Deny	Deny	Deny
14) Christ's Second Coming	Accept	Deny	Deny	Deny

◆ Accept   ▲ Redefine   ● Deny

Hear O Israel: The Lord our God, the Lord is one! —Deuteronomy 6:4

I am the Lord your God.... You shall have no other gods before Me. —Exodus 20:2-3

Before me no god was formed, nor will there be one after me. I, even I, am the Lord and apart from me there is no savior. —Isaiah 43:10-11

God's Tri-unity

While there is only one God, he exists eternally in three Persons. In the Bible —
- the Father is called God,
  (2 Thessalonians 1:2)
- the Son (Jesus) is called God,
  (John 1:1-5; John 10:30-33; John 20:28; Hebrews 1:8; Philippians 2:9-11)
- the Holy Spirit is called God.
  (Acts 5:3-4, 2 Corinthians 3:17)

He is one substance but three Persons in relationship. There are more than 60 passages in the Bible that mention the three Persons together.

What Do I Actually Need to Believe?
God is one essence, but three Persons.

What's at Stake Here?
The unity and relational nature of God.

As soon as Jesus was baptized, he went up out of the water. At that moment heaven was opened, and he saw the Spirit of God descending like a dove and lighting on him. And a voice from heaven said, "This is my Son, whom I love; with him I am well pleased'." —Matthew 3:16, 17

Therefore go and make disciples of all nations, baptizing them in the name of the Father and of the Son and of the Holy Spirit.... —Matthew 28:19

May the grace of the Lord Jesus Christ, and the love of God, and the fellowship of the Holy Spirit be with you all. —2 Corinthians 13:14

Human Depravity

Since God is a personal Being, he wants personal relationships with human beings.
Human depravity means that every human is spiritually separated from God, totally incapable of saving himself. When Adam sinned, he died spiritually and his relationship with God was severed. Additionally, all of Adam's descendants are "dead in trespasses" (Ephesians 2:1). Without a new birth (being created anew) no one can enter life (John 3:3).

11. CHRIST'S BODILY RESURRECTION

The atoning death of Christ paid for our sins, but the process was not complete until he had defeated death by being physically resurrected in the same body (John 2:19-21). Because Christ is the victor over death and the prototype of a new, glorified physical body, all of humanity will be resurrected and live forever in either heaven or hell.

What Do I Actually Need to Believe?
Jesus rose bodily from the grave.

What's at Stake Here?
The proof that Jesus conquered death.

He was delivered over to death for our sins and was raised to life for our justification. —Romans 4:25

… if you confess with your mouth, "Jesus is Lord," and believe in your heart that God raised him from the dead, you will be saved. —Romans 10:9

Touch me and see; a ghost does not have flesh and bones, as you see I have. —Luke 24:39

12. CHRIST'S BODILY ASCENSION

Christ died for our sins and was physically resurrected for our salvation. Then 40 days later, he was taken up ("ascended") bodily into heaven. Because Christ has ascended to the Father, the Holy Spirit now guides us, shows us where we are wrong and comforts us when we hurt. Jesus' going to the Father means our life is kept safe in heaven with God.

What Do I Actually Need to Believe?
Jesus ascended, body and soul, to God.

10 CHRIST'S ATONING DEATH

The penalty for sin is death—not only physical death (separation of the soul from the body), but also spiritual death (separation of ourselves from God). The penalty we owe to God was paid by Christ through his death on the cross. The acceptable payment had to be perfect, complete, and without fault. Christ, the perfect Man, gave Himself in our place, so that whoever believes in him will not die (physically and spiritually) but have everlasting life (John 3:16).

What Do I Actually Need to Believe?
Only Christ's sinless life, sacrificial death and bodily resurrection can bring us to God.

What's at Stake Here?
The unique nature of Jesus' work of salvation.

For even the Son of Man did not come to be served, but to serve, and to give his life as a ransom for many. —Mark 10:45

He himself bore our sins in his body on the tree, so that we might die to sins and live for righteousness. —1 Peter 2:24

For Christ died for sins once for all, the righteous for the unrighteous, to bring you to God. —1 Peter 3:18

No one comes to the Father except through me. —John 14:6

ROSE PUBLISHING

© 2007 Norman L. Geisler
Published by Rose Publishing, Inc.
4733 Torrance Blvd., #259
Torrance, CA 90503 U.S.A.
email: info@rose-publishing.com
www.rose-publishing.com

All rights reserved. It is illegal to copy, transmit electronically, or reproduce this pamphlet in whole or in part in any form. 060713SCG
Printed in the USA. May not be posted or transmitted on the internet.

Norman L. Geisler, M.A., Th.B., Ph.D., is the founder and Dean of Southern Evangelical Seminary and the Veritas Graduate School of Apologetics. He is author of numerous books on apologetics and theology, many of which are considered "standard texts" in Christian colleges throughout the world.
Special thanks to Shawn Vander Lugt and William Brent Ashby.

All Scripture quotations, unless otherwise indicated, are taken from the *Holy Bible, New International Version*®. NIV®. Copyright © 1973, 1978, 1984 by International Bible Society. Used by permission of Zondervan. All rights reserved.

Stock #609X *Essential Doctrine Made Easy* pamphlet
Retailers: Package of 5 pamphlets = Stock #610X (ISBN-13: 978-159636-144-7)